I0017123

Social Media Success: Instagram, YouTube, and Monetization Secrets

by

Mega Influencer

Vishal Raj Oberoi

Social Media Success: Instagram, YouTube, and Monetization Secrets with Vishal Raj Oberoi

Chapter 1: Introduction to Social Media Influence

- Defining social media influencers

- The rise of influencer marketing

- Why becoming an influencer is a viable career option

Chapter 2: Building Your Personal Brand

- Identifying your niche and target audience

- Crafting a compelling personal brand story

- Creating a cohesive aesthetic across platforms

Chapter 3: Mastering Instagram

- Optimizing your Instagram profile

- Content creation strategies for Instagram

- Growing your followers organically

- Leveraging Instagram features like IGTV, Reels, and Stories

Chapter 4: Conquering YouTube

- Setting up a successful YouTube channel

- Developing engaging video content

- Growing your subscriber base

- Monetization options on YouTube: AdSense, sponsored content, merchandise, memberships, etc.

Chapter 5: Collaboration and Networking

- The importance of networking with other influencers and brands

- Collaborating with other influencers for mutual benefit

- Building relationships with brands for sponsored content opportunities

Chapter 6: Monetization Strategies

- Understanding different revenue streams for influencers

- Sponsored content and brand partnerships

- Affiliate marketing and sponsorships

- Selling digital products or merchandise

- Creating exclusive content for premium subscribers

Chapter 7: Managing Your Finances

- Budgeting and managing income as an influencer

- Tax considerations for influencers

- Hiring professionals (accountants, lawyers, etc.) when needed

Chapter 8: Dealing with Challenges and Controversies

- Handling negative comments and online trolls

- Navigating algorithm changes on social media platforms

- Dealing with burnout and maintaining mental health

Chapter 9: Staying Relevant and Evolving

- Keeping up with trends in social media and influencer marketing

- Adapting your content strategy over time

- Diversifying your income streams to mitigate risk

Chapter 10: Looking to the Future

- Predictions for the future of influencer marketing

- Advice for aspiring influencers entering the field

Chapter 1: Introduction to Social Media Influence

In today's digital era, social media has revolutionized the way people interact, share information, and make decisions. At the forefront of this digital revolution are social media influencers, individuals who have amassed significant followings and wield considerable influence over their audience's opinions, behaviors, and purchasing choices.

- ## Defining Social Media Influencers

Social media influencers are individuals who have cultivated a dedicated and engaged following on platforms like Instagram, YouTube, TikTok, and Twitter. They leverage their online presence to create and share content that resonates with their audience, often focusing on specific niches such as fashion, beauty, fitness, travel, or lifestyle. What distinguishes influencers is their ability to authentically connect with their followers, earning their trust and loyalty through consistent, relatable content.

- ## The Rise of Influencer Marketing

In recent years, influencer marketing has emerged as a dominant force in the advertising industry. Brands are increasingly collaborating with influencers to promote their products and services to a highly targeted audience. Unlike traditional advertising methods, influencer marketing offers a more authentic and organic way for brands to connect with consumers. By partnering with influencers who align with their values and target demographics, brands can leverage the influencer's credibility and authenticity to drive engagement, brand awareness, and ultimately, sales.

- ## Why Becoming an Influencer is a Viable Career Option

The allure of becoming an influencer extends beyond just fame and recognition; it has also become a viable career path for many individuals. Here are several reasons why:

1. Creative Expression: Influencers have the freedom to express themselves creatively and share their passions with a global audience. Whether it's through photography, videography, writing, or other forms of content creation, influencers can showcase their unique talents and perspectives.

2. Flexibility and Independence: As an influencer, you have the flexibility to work on your own terms and schedule. You can create content from anywhere in the world, allowing for a lifestyle that prioritizes freedom and independence.

3. Monetization Opportunities: Influencers have various avenues to monetize their online presence, including sponsored content, brand partnerships, affiliate marketing, product collaborations, and even launching their own products or services. With the right strategy, influencers can generate substantial income streams from their social media platforms.

4. Community Building: Influencers have the opportunity to build genuine connections with their followers and foster a sense of community around their content. By engaging with their audience through comments, DMs, and live interactions, influencers can create a loyal fan base that values their content and recommendations.

5. Personal Branding: Becoming an influencer allows individuals to cultivate a personal brand that reflects their interests, values, and expertise. A strong personal brand not only attracts followers but also opens doors to various professional opportunities, including partnerships, collaborations, and speaking engagements.

6. In conclusion, social media influencers play a significant role in shaping consumer behavior, driving trends, and influencing purchasing decisions in today's digital landscape. As influencer marketing continues to evolve and mature, the opportunities for individuals to build successful careers as influencers are abundant. By leveraging their creativity, authenticity, and strategic partnerships, aspiring influencers can turn their passion for content creation into a lucrative and fulfilling profession.

Chapter 2: Building Your Personal Brand

Your personal brand is the foundation of your influence as a social media influencer. It's what sets you apart from others and defines how your audience perceives you. In this chapter, we'll explore key strategies for building a strong and compelling personal brand.

- ## Identifying Your Niche and Target Audience

1. Define Your Niche: Start by identifying your passion, expertise, or area of interest. What topics or subjects are you most knowledgeable about or enthusiastic about sharing with others? Your niche should be specific enough to differentiate you from others but broad enough to attract a sizable audience.

2. Research Your Target Audience: Understand who your target audience is and what they're looking for. What demographics do they belong to? What are their interests, pain points, and preferences? Conduct surveys, analyze your existing followers, and engage with your audience to gain insights into their needs and preferences.

3. Align Your Content with Audience Needs: Once you have a clear understanding of your niche and target audience, tailor your content to meet their needs and interests. Provide valuable, relevant, and engaging content that resonates with your audience and establishes you as a credible authority in your niche.

- ## Crafting a Compelling Personal Brand Story

1. Define Your Brand Values: What do you stand for? What are your core values, beliefs, and principles? Your personal brand should reflect your authentic self and what you stand for. Define your brand values and use them as a guiding framework for your content and interactions with your audience.

2. Tell Your Story: Share your personal journey, experiences, and lessons learned. Your personal brand story should be authentic, relatable, and inspiring. Use storytelling techniques to connect with your audience on an emotional level and establish a deeper connection with them.

3. Consistency and Authenticity: Be consistent in your messaging, tone, and visual identity across all your social media platforms. Authenticity is key to building trust and credibility with your audience. Be genuine, transparent, and true to yourself in everything you do.

- ## Creating a Cohesive Aesthetic Across Platforms

1. Visual Branding: Develop a cohesive visual identity that reflects your personal brand and resonates with your audience. This includes your logo, color palette, typography,

and imagery. Use consistent visual elements across all your social media platforms to create a cohesive brand experience.

2. Branding Guidelines: Create branding guidelines or style guides to maintain consistency in your visual branding. Outline specific rules and guidelines for using your brand colors, fonts, logos, and imagery. This ensures that your brand remains consistent and recognizable across all platforms.

3. Curate Your Content: Curate your content to align with your visual branding and aesthetic. Pay attention to the composition, colors, and overall look and feel of your content. Use editing tools and filters to maintain a consistent visual style and aesthetic across your feed.

By identifying your niche, crafting a compelling personal brand story, and creating a cohesive aesthetic across platforms, you can establish a strong and memorable personal brand that resonates with your audience and sets you apart as a social media influencer.

Chapter 3: Mastering Instagram

Instagram has become one of the most influential social media platforms for content creators and influencers. In this chapter, we'll delve into key strategies for mastering Instagram, including optimizing your profile, content creation strategies, growing your followers organically, and leveraging Instagram features like Reels and Stories.

• Optimizing Your Instagram Profile

1. Profile Picture: Choose a clear, high-quality profile picture that represents your personal brand or your niche. This could be a professional headshot or a logo that reflects your brand identity.

2. Bio: Craft a compelling bio that succinctly describes who you are, what you do, and what your audience can expect from your content. Use keywords and hashtags relevant to your niche to make your profile more discoverable.

3. Link in Bio: Utilize the link in your bio to direct traffic to your website, blog, YouTube channel, or any other external content you want to promote. You can also use tools like Linktree to create a custom landing page with multiple links.

4. Highlight Covers: Create custom highlight covers for your Instagram Stories highlights to make your profile visually

appealing and organized. Use consistent branding elements to maintain a cohesive aesthetic.

- ## Content Creation Strategies for Instagram

1. Visual Aesthetic: Develop a consistent visual aesthetic for your Instagram feed. This could include using a specific color palette, editing style, or theme that reflects your brand identity. Use editing tools like Lightroom or VSCO to enhance your photos and maintain a cohesive look.

2. Content Mix: Diversify your content mix to keep your audience engaged. Share a variety of content formats, including photos, videos, carousels, and Stories. Experiment with different types of content to see what resonates best with your audience.

3. Storytelling: Use storytelling techniques to create engaging captions that accompany your posts. Share personal anecdotes, behind-the-scenes insights, or motivational messages to connect with your audience on a deeper level.

4. User-Generated Content: Encourage user-generated content by featuring your followers' photos or videos on your feed or Stories. This not only fosters a sense of community but also provides fresh content and social proof for your brand.

- ## Growing Your Followers Organically

1. Engagement: Actively engage with your audience by responding to comments, DMs, and mentions. Engage with other users' content by liking, commenting, and sharing posts within your niche.

2. Hashtags: Use relevant hashtags to make your posts more discoverable to users interested in your niche. Research popular and niche-specific hashtags and incorporate them strategically into your posts.

3. Collaborations: Collaborate with other influencers or brands within your niche to reach a wider audience and gain exposure. Participate in Instagram challenges, shoutout exchanges, or joint giveaways to attract new followers.

4. Consistency: Post consistently and at optimal times to maintain visibility and engagement. Use Instagram Insights to analyze your audience's activity and determine the best times to post for maximum reach.

- ## Leveraging Instagram Features like Reels and Stories

1. Instagram Reels: Create short, entertaining video content using Instagram Reels to showcase your personality, creativity, and expertise. Experiment with trending sounds, effects, and challenges to increase engagement and reach.

2. Instagram Stories: Use Instagram Stories to share behind-the scenes content, updates, and sneak peeks with your audience. Take advantage of interactive features like polls, questions, and quizzes to encourage engagement and feedback.

3. Highlights: Save your Stories as Highlights on your profile to showcase important or evergreen content. Organize your Highlights into categories or themes to make it easier for users to navigate and explore your content.

By optimizing your Instagram profile, implementing effective content creation strategies, growing your followers organically, and leveraging Instagram features like Reels and Stories, you can master Instagram as a social media influencer and connect with your audience in meaningful ways.

Chapter 4: Conquering YouTube

YouTube has emerged as a powerhouse platform for content creators and influencers, offering immense opportunities for sharing video content, building communities, and monetizing your passion. In this chapter, we'll explore key strategies for conquering YouTube, including setting up a successful channel, developing engaging video content, growing your subscriber base, and exploring monetization options.

- ## Setting Up a Successful YouTube Channel

1. Create a Channel: Start by creating a YouTube channel with a clear and memorable name that reflects your brand or niche. Customize your channel layout, banner, and profile picture to make a strong first impression.

2. Optimize Your Channel: Optimize your channel metadata, including your channel description, keywords, and tags, to improve discoverability and search rankings. Use relevant keywords related to your niche to attract your target audience.

3. Upload Consistently: Develop a consistent upload schedule and stick to it. Regularly upload high-quality content to keep your audience engaged and coming back for more.

4. Engage with Your Audience: Foster a sense of community on your channel by responding to comments, engaging with your audience in the comments section, and encouraging discussion and feedback.

• Developing Engaging Video Content

1. Know Your Audience: Understand your audience's interests, preferences, and pain points. Create content that addresses their needs and provides value to them.

2. Plan Your Content: Plan your video content in advance and create a content calendar to stay organized. Brainstorm ideas, outline your videos, and consider incorporating different formats such as tutorials, vlogs, reviews, and challenges.

3. Quality Production: Invest in high-quality equipment, including a good camera, microphone, and lighting setup, to ensure professional-looking videos. Pay attention to audio quality, video resolution, and editing to create polished content.

4. Tell Compelling Stories: Use storytelling techniques to capture your audience's attention and keep them engaged throughout your videos. Structure your content with a clear beginning, middle, and end, and incorporate elements like anecdotes, humor, and suspense to captivate your viewers.

• Growing Your Subscriber Base

1. Promote Your Channel: Promote your channel on other social media platforms, your website, and through collaborations with other YouTubers or influencers in your niche. Cross-promotion can help attract new subscribers and expand your audience.

2. Optimize for Search: Optimize your video titles, descriptions, and tags with relevant keywords to improve your video's visibility in YouTube search results and suggested videos.

3. Encourage Subscriptions: Encourage viewers to subscribe to your channel by including a call-to-action at the beginning or end of your videos. Offer incentives such as exclusive content, giveaways, or shoutouts to incentivize subscriptions.

4. Engage with Your Community: Build rapport with your audience by actively engaging with them through comments, live streams, and community posts. Show appreciation for your subscribers and create a welcoming and supportive environment on your channel.

- Monetization Options on YouTube

1. AdSense: Enable monetization on your channel to earn money through ads displayed on your videos. You can earn revenue based on the number of views and ad interactions your videos receive.

2. Sponsored Content: Collaborate with brands to create sponsored content that promotes their products or services. Negotiate sponsored deals directly with brands or join influencer marketing platforms to connect with potential sponsors.

3. Merchandise: Create and sell your own merchandise, such as t-shirts, hats, or accessories, to your audience. Use platforms like Teespring or Spreadshop to design and sell custom merchandise directly from your channel.

4. Memberships: Offer channel memberships to your subscribers, providing exclusive perks such as access to members-only content, custom badges, and emojis. Subscribers can support your channel through monthly memberships in exchange for special benefits.

5. Affiliate Marketing: Promote affiliate products or services in your videos and earn a commission for every sale or referral generated through your unique affiliate links. Choose affiliate products that align with your niche and provide value to your audience.

By setting up a successful YouTube channel, developing engaging video content, growing your subscriber base, and exploring monetization options, you can conquer YouTube as a content creator and build a profitable and sustainable career on the platform.

Chapter 5: Collaboration and Networking

In the competitive landscape of social media, collaboration and networking are indispensable tools for expanding your reach, fostering meaningful connections, and unlocking new opportunities. In this chapter, we'll explore the significance of networking with other influencers and brands, collaborating with fellow creators for mutual benefit, and building relationships with brands for sponsored content opportunities.

- ## The Importance of Networking with Other Influencers and Brands

1. Expand Your Reach: Networking with other influencers and brands exposes you to new audiences and potential followers who may share similar interests or demographics. Collaborating with influencers or brands with complementary audiences can help you reach a wider and more diverse audience.

2. Exchange Knowledge and Expertise: Networking allows you to connect with industry peers and exchange valuable insights, tips, and strategies. By learning from others' experiences and expertise, you can gain new perspectives and refine your own approach to content creation and influencer marketing.

3. Support and Collaboration: Building relationships with other influencers fosters a sense of community and support within

the influencer ecosystem. Collaborating on projects, cross-promoting each other's content, or sharing resources and opportunities can benefit all parties involved and strengthen the influencer community as a whole.

- ## Collaborating with Other Influencers for Mutual Benefit

1. Identify Compatible Partners: When seeking collaboration opportunities, look for influencers whose audience, niche, and values align with yours. Consider factors such as audience demographics, content style, and engagement levels to ensure compatibility and mutual benefit.

2. Explore Different Collaboration Formats: Collaborations can take various forms, including co-hosting a live stream, participating in a joint challenge or series, creating guest appearances or shoutouts, or collaborating on a sponsored campaign. Be creative and open to experimenting with different collaboration formats to keep your content fresh and engaging.

3. Communicate Clearly and Set Expectations: When initiating collaborations, clearly communicate your goals, expectations, and requirements with your potential collaborators. Establish a timeline, outline roles and responsibilities, and discuss compensation or benefits upfront to avoid misunderstandings or conflicts later on.

- Building Relationships with Brands for Sponsored Content Opportunities

1. Research and Target Brands: Identify brands that align with your niche, audience, and personal brand values. Research potential brand partners, their products or services, and their existing influencer partnerships to determine if there's a good fit.

2. Create Compelling Pitch Materials: Develop a professional media kit or pitch deck that showcases your audience demographics, engagement metrics, past collaborations, and the value you can offer to potential brand partners. Tailor your pitch materials to each brand and highlight how collaborating with you can help achieve their marketing objectives.

3. Establish Trust and Authenticity: Brands value authenticity and credibility in their influencer partnerships. Build trust with brands by maintaining transparency, delivering high-quality content, and aligning your sponsored content with your authentic voice and values. Authenticity resonates with audiences and enhances the effectiveness of sponsored campaigns.

4. Nurture Long-Term Relationships: Foster positive and long-term relationships with brands by delivering on your commitments, providing exceptional service, and demonstrating professionalism and reliability. Cultivate trust and loyalty with brands to increase the likelihood of repeat collaborations and ongoing partnerships.

By actively networking with other influencers and brands, collaborating on mutually beneficial projects, and building strong relationships with brands for sponsored content opportunities, you can expand your influence, unlock new opportunities, and achieve sustainable growth as a social media influencer.

Chapter 6: Monetization Strategies

As a social media influencer, monetizing your online presence is essential for turning your passion into a sustainable and profitable career. In this chapter, we'll explore various monetization strategies that influencers can leverage to generate revenue, including sponsored content and brand partnerships, affiliate marketing, selling digital products or merchandise, and creating exclusive content for premium subscribers.

- ## Understanding Different Revenue Streams for Influencers

1. Sponsored Content and Brand Partnerships: Collaborating with brands to create sponsored content is one of the most common and lucrative monetization strategies for influencers. Brands pay influencers to promote their products or services to their audience through sponsored posts, videos, or other forms of content.

2. Affiliate Marketing: Affiliate marketing involves promoting third-party products or services and earning a commission for every sale or referral generated through your unique affiliate links. Influencers can partner with affiliate programs relevant to their niche and promote products they genuinely recommend to their audience.

3. Selling Digital Products or Merchandise: Influencers can create and sell digital products such as e-books, online courses, presets, or templates tailored to their audience's interests and needs.

Additionally, influencers can design and sell branded merchandise, such as apparel, accessories, or merchandise related to their niche.

4. Creating Exclusive Content for Premium Subscribers: Some influencers offer premium subscription services or membership programs that provide exclusive access to gated content, behind-the-scenes footage, private communities, or personalized perks. Subscribers pay a recurring fee to access premium content and support their favorite influencers.

- ## Sponsored Content and Brand Partnerships

1. Identify Suitable Brands: Partner with brands whose products or services align with your niche, audience, and personal brand values. Conduct research to identify potential brand partners and reach out to them with a compelling pitch highlighting the value you can offer as an influencer.

2. Negotiate Terms and Compensation: Negotiate terms and compensation for sponsored collaborations, including deliverables, timeline, exclusivity, and payment structure. Consider factors such as your audience reach, engagement metrics, and the scope of work when determining your rates.

3. Disclose Sponsored Content: Adhere to FTC guidelines and disclose sponsored content transparently to your audience. Clearly indicate when content is sponsored, whether through hashtags like #ad, #sponsored, or by including a disclosure within the content itself.

- ## Affiliate Marketing and Sponsorships

1. Choose Relevant Affiliate Programs: Join affiliate programs that offer products or services relevant to your niche and audience. Research and select reputable affiliate programs with high-quality products, competitive commissions, and reliable tracking and reporting systems.

2. Promote Affiliate Products Authentically: Promote affiliate products authentically by incorporating them naturally into your content and providing genuine recommendations and reviews. Focus on products you genuinely believe in and that offer value to your audience.

3. Track and Optimize Performance: Monitor your affiliate marketing performance closely and track key metrics such as click-through rates, conversion rates, and commission earnings. Optimize your affiliate marketing strategy based on performance data and experiment with different promotional tactics to maximize revenue.

- ## Selling Digital Products or Merchandise

1. Create High-Quality Digital Products: Develop high-quality digital products such as e-books, online courses, or digital downloads that provide value and address your audience's needs or interests. Invest time and effort into creating

compelling content and designing visually appealing products.

2. Promote Your Products Effectively: Promote your digital products or merchandise through various channels, including your social media platforms, website, email newsletter, and collaborations with other influencers or brands. Utilize persuasive copywriting, visual assets, and calls-to-action to encourage conversions.

3. Offer Discounts or Limited-Time Offers: Encourage sales and incentivize purchases by offering discounts, special promotions, or limited-time offers on your digital products or merchandise. Create a sense of urgency and exclusivity to motivate your audience to take action.

- ## Creating Exclusive Content for Premium Subscribers

1. Define Subscription Tiers and Benefits: Determine subscription tiers and benefits based on the value you can offer to premium subscribers. Offer exclusive access to premium content, behind-the-scenes footage, private communities, Q&A sessions, or personalized interactions as incentives for subscribing.

2. Set Subscription Pricing: Set subscription pricing that reflects the value of the premium content and perks you provide. Consider factors such as the quality and uniqueness

of the content, the frequency of updates, and the level of engagement and interaction with subscribers.

3. Promote Your Subscription Service: Promote your premium subscription service across your social media platforms, website, email newsletter, and other marketing channels. Highlight the benefits and value proposition of subscribing and encourage your audience to become premium members.

By diversifying your monetization strategies and leveraging multiple revenue streams, influencers can create sustainable income streams and build a thriving career in the digital space. Experiment with different monetization methods, adapt to evolving trends and consumer preferences, and prioritize providing value to your audience to maximize your earning potential as an influencer.

Chapter 7: Managing Your Finances

Managing your finances effectively is crucial for long-term success and sustainability as an influencer. In this chapter, we'll explore key aspects of financial management for influencers, including budgeting and managing income, tax considerations, and the importance of hiring professionals when needed.

- ## Budgeting and Managing Income as an Influencer

1. Create a Budget: Establish a budget to track your income and expenses effectively. Allocate funds for essential expenses such as equipment, software subscriptions, marketing, and professional services, as well as savings and investments for future growth and stability.

2. Track Your Income Sources: Keep detailed records of your income sources, including earnings from sponsored content, affiliate marketing, merchandise sales, and premium subscriptions. Use accounting software or spreadsheets to organize your income streams and monitor your financial performance over time.

3. Manage Expenses Wisely: Be mindful of your expenses and prioritize spending on investments that contribute to your growth and success as an influencer. Evaluate the return on investment (ROI) of your expenses and avoid unnecessary or frivolous spending that does not align with your goals.

4. Plan for Fluctuating Income: Recognize that income as an influencer can vary from month to month due to factors such as fluctuating engagement, seasonal trends, and changes in sponsorship opportunities. Build a financial cushion by saving a portion of your earnings during peak months to cover expenses during slower periods.

- ## Tax Considerations for Influencers

1. Understand Tax Obligations: Familiarize yourself with the tax obligations and requirements for influencers in your jurisdiction. As a self-employed individual, you may be responsible for paying income tax, self-employment tax, and potentially other taxes such as sales tax or VAT on digital products.

2. Keep Accurate Records: Maintain accurate records of your income, expenses, and receipts throughout the year to facilitate tax preparation and reporting. Use accounting software or hire a bookkeeper to track your finances and ensure compliance with tax regulations.

3. Deductible Expenses: Take advantage of tax deductions available to influencers, such as business expenses related to equipment, software, travel, marketing, and professional services. Consult with a tax professional to identify eligible deductions and maximize your tax savings.

4. Quarterly Estimated Taxes: If you expect to owe more than a certain amount in taxes annually, you may be required to make quarterly estimated tax payments to the IRS or relevant tax authorities. Estimate your tax liability accurately and make timely quarterly payments to avoid penalties and interest.

- ## Hiring Professionals When Needed

1. Accountants: Consider hiring an accountant or tax professional with experience working with influencers to help you navigate complex tax regulations, maximize deductions, and ensure compliance with tax laws. An accountant can also provide valuable financial advice and help you optimize your financial strategy.

2. Lawyers: Seek legal advice from a lawyer specializing in influencer marketing and intellectual property law to protect your rights and interests. A lawyer can assist with contract review and negotiation, trademark and copyright registration, dispute resolution, and other legal matters relevant to influencers.

3. Financial Advisors: Consult with a financial advisor or wealth manager to develop a comprehensive financial plan tailored to your goals, risk tolerance, and financial situation. A financial advisor can provide guidance on investment strategies, retirement planning, insurance coverage, and wealth preservation strategies.

4. Business Managers: Consider hiring a business manager or financial planner to oversee your financial affairs and help you make informed decisions about budgeting, investing, and strategic planning. A business manager can handle administrative tasks, financial analysis, and day-to-day financial operations, allowing you to focus on creating content and growing your brand.

By implementing sound financial management practices, understanding your tax obligations, and seeking professional advice when needed, you can effectively manage your finances as an influencer and build a solid foundation for long-term financial success and stability. Prioritize financial literacy, invest in professional support when necessary, and proactively manage your finances to achieve your goals as an influencer.

Chapter 8: Dealing with Challenges and Controversies

As an influencer navigating the digital landscape, you're bound to encounter challenges and controversies along the way. In this chapter, we'll explore strategies for handling negative comments and online trolls, navigating algorithm changes on social media platforms, and dealing with burnout while prioritizing your mental health.

- ## Handling Negative Comments and Online Trolls

1. Develop Resilience: Recognize that negative comments and online trolls are unfortunately part of the territory in the digital world. Build resilience by reframing negative feedback as opportunities for growth and learning rather than personal attacks.

2. Set Boundaries: Establish boundaries for yourself and your online interactions. Decide how much time and energy you're willing to devote to engaging with negative comments and trolls, and don't hesitate to block or mute individuals who consistently spread negativity.

3. Focus on Positive Engagement: Shift your focus towards positive engagement with your audience and supporters. Prioritize responding to constructive feedback, fostering meaningful conversations, and building a supportive community around your content.

4. Seek Support: Lean on your support network of friends, family, and fellow influencers for emotional support and perspective during challenging times. Don't hesitate to reach out for help or guidance if you're feeling overwhelmed or distressed by negative comments.

- ## Navigating Algorithm Changes on Social Media Platforms

1. Stay Informed: Stay informed about algorithm changes and updates on social media platforms by following official announcements, reading industry news, and participating in online communities and forums where influencers discuss trends and best practices.

2. Adapt Your Strategy: Be adaptable and flexible in your content strategy to accommodate algorithm changes and fluctuations in engagement. Experiment with different types of content, posting frequencies, and engagement tactics to optimize your performance on social media platforms.

3. Diversify Your Platforms: Diversify your presence across multiple social media platforms to mitigate the impact of algorithm changes on any single platform. Build a presence on platforms where your audience is active and engage with them through various channels.

4. Focus on Quality Content: Prioritize creating high-quality, engaging content that resonates with your audience and encourages meaningful interactions. Algorithms tend to favor content that generates positive engagement and keeps users on the platform for longer periods.

- ## Dealing with Burnout and Maintaining Mental Health

1. Practice Self-Care: Prioritize self-care and make time for activities that recharge and rejuvenate you outside of your influencer duties. Practice mindfulness, exercise regularly, spend time with loved ones, and pursue hobbies and interests unrelated to social media.

2. Set Realistic Expectations: Manage your workload and set realistic expectations for yourself in terms of content creation, posting frequency, and engagement. Avoid overcommitting or spreading yourself too thin, and delegate tasks or outsource responsibilities when necessary.

3. Take Breaks When Needed: Recognize when you need to take breaks from social media to recharge and prevent burnout. Schedule regular breaks or "social media detoxes" to disconnect from the online world and focus on your well-being.

4. Seek Professional Help: If you're struggling with burnout, anxiety, or other mental health challenges, don't hesitate to seek professional help from a therapist, counselor, or mental

health professional. Therapy can provide valuable support and coping strategies for managing stress and maintaining mental wellness.

By implementing strategies for handling negative comments, navigating algorithm changes, and prioritizing your mental health, you can effectively navigate challenges and controversies as an influencer while staying true to yourself and your values. Remember to prioritize self-care, seek support when needed, and maintain a healthy perspective on your online presence and influence.

Chapter 9: Staying Relevant and Evolving

In the fast-paced world of social media and influencer marketing, staying relevant and evolving with the landscape is essential for long-term success. In this chapter, we'll explore strategies for keeping up with trends in social media and influencer marketing, adapting your content strategy over time, and diversifying your income streams to mitigate risk.

- ## Keeping Up with Trends in Social Media and Influencer Marketing

1. Continuous Learning: Stay informed about emerging trends, new features, and best practices in social media and influencer marketing through industry publications, online resources, webinars, and conferences. Follow thought leaders and influencers in your niche to stay abreast of the latest developments.

2. Monitor Platform Updates: Keep an eye on platform updates and algorithm changes on social media platforms to adapt your strategy accordingly. Stay informed about new features, content formats, and trends that can enhance your visibility and engagement on each platform.

3. Engage with Your Audience: Actively engage with your audience to gather insights, feedback, and preferences. Conduct polls, surveys, and Q&A sessions to understand

what content resonates with your audience and adjust your strategy based on their interests and preferences.

4. Experiment and Innovate: Be open to experimentation and innovation in your content strategy. Test new formats, trends, and ideas to keep your content fresh and engaging. Don't be afraid to step outside your comfort zone and try new approaches to connect with your audience.

• Adapting Your Content Strategy Over Time

1. Evaluate Performance Metrics: Regularly analyze performance metrics such as engagement, reach, and conversion rates to assess the effectiveness of your content strategy. Identify trends, patterns, and areas for improvement to refine your approach over time.

2. Stay Flexible and Agile: Remain flexible and agile in response to changes in audience preferences, platform dynamics, and industry trends. Be willing to pivot your content strategy as needed to capitalize on emerging opportunities and address evolving challenges.

3. Listen to Feedback: Listen to feedback from your audience, peers, and industry experts to identify areas where you can improve and innovate. Take constructive criticism in stride and use it as an opportunity for growth and refinement.

4. Evolve Your Brand Identity: As your audience grows and evolves, so should your brand identity and content strategy. Continuously refine your brand messaging, visual identity, and content themes to stay relevant and resonate with your audience.

• Diversifying Your Income Streams to Mitigate Risk

1. Explore Multiple Revenue Streams: Diversify your income streams beyond sponsored content to mitigate risk and enhance financial stability. Explore opportunities such as affiliate marketing, digital products, merchandise sales, premium subscriptions, and speaking engagements.

2. Balance Short-Term and Long-Term Gains: Strike a balance between short-term revenue opportunities and long-term investments in building sustainable income streams. Prioritize investments that provide recurring revenue or passive income to create a more stable financial foundation.

3. Plan for Contingencies: Anticipate potential disruptions or downturns in your primary income streams and have contingency plans in place to mitigate their impact. Build a financial buffer or emergency fund to weather unforeseen challenges or changes in the industry.

4. Stay Agile and Adaptive: Remain agile and adaptive in response to changes in the market and evolving consumer behaviors. Be proactive in identifying new income

opportunities and diversifying your revenue streams to stay resilient in the face of uncertainty.

By staying informed about trends in social media and influencer marketing, adapting your content strategy over time, and diversifying your income streams, you can stay relevant, resilient, and successful in the ever-changing landscape of digital influence. Embrace change as an opportunity for growth, innovation, and evolution, and continue to refine your approach to thrive as an influencer in the years to come.

Chapter 10: Looking to the Future

As influencer marketing continues to evolve and shape the digital landscape, it's essential to anticipate future trends and prepare for what lies ahead. In this chapter, we'll explore predictions for the future of influencer marketing and offer advice for aspiring influencers entering the field.

- ## Predictions for the Future of Influencer Marketing

1. Rise of Micro and Nano Influencers: As consumers crave authenticity and relatability, there will be a shift towards micro and nano influencers who have smaller but highly engaged audiences. Brands will prioritize working with influencers who can create genuine connections and drive meaningful engagement with their audience.

2. Video Dominance: Video content will continue to dominate social media platforms, with short-form videos, live streams, and interactive content becoming increasingly popular. Influencers who can create compelling video content will have a competitive edge in capturing audience attention and driving engagement.

3. Emergence of New Platforms: As social media platforms evolve and new platforms emerge, influencers will need to adapt and diversify their presence across multiple channels. Emerging platforms such as TikTok, Clubhouse, and

emerging social commerce platforms will offer new opportunities for influencers to connect with audiences and monetize their content.

4. Authenticity and Transparency: Authenticity and transparency will remain paramount in influencer marketing, with consumers demanding genuine connections and honest recommendations from influencers. Influencers who prioritize authenticity, transparency, and ethical practices will build trust and credibility with their audience and brands.

5. Data-Driven Influencer Marketing: Brands will increasingly rely on data and analytics to inform influencer marketing strategies and measure campaign performance. Influencers who can provide actionable insights and demonstrate the impact of their collaborations through data-driven metrics will be in high demand.

- ## Advice for Aspiring Influencers Entering the Field

1. Find Your Niche: Identify your unique strengths, passions, and interests, and carve out a niche for yourself within the influencer landscape. Focus on a specific topic or niche where you can provide value and establish yourself as an authority or expert.

2. Build Your Personal Brand: Invest time and effort into building a strong and compelling personal brand that resonates with your target audience. Define your brand identity, voice, and values, and consistently communicate them across your content and interactions.

3. Create Quality Content: Prioritize creating high-quality, engaging content that showcases your creativity, expertise, and personality. Experiment with different formats, styles, and platforms to find what resonates best with your audience and sets you apart from others.

4. Engage and Network: Actively engage with your audience and network with fellow influencers, brands, and industry professionals. Build genuine relationships, collaborate on projects, and leverage networking opportunities to expand your reach and grow your influence.

5. Stay Resilient and Persistent: Success as an influencer takes time, dedication, and persistence. Be prepared to face challenges, setbacks, and rejection along the way, but stay resilient and committed to your goals. Stay true to yourself, stay focused on your passion, and keep pushing forward even in the face of adversity.

As you embark on your journey as an influencer, remember to stay adaptable, open to change, and committed to continuous learning and growth. Embrace the evolving landscape of influencer marketing, stay true to your authentic voice and values, and keep striving to make a positive impact on your audience and the world around you.

As I reflect on my journey as an influencer, I am filled with gratitude for the opportunities, challenges, and growth that have shaped my path. From humble beginnings to building a thriving online presence, my journey has been a testament to the power of passion, perseverance, and authenticity in the digital age.

Embarking on your own influencer journey is an exhilarating and rewarding experience, but it's also filled with uncertainties, obstacles, and moments of self-doubt. As you navigate the ever-changing landscape of social media and influencer marketing, I offer you the following words of encouragement and advice:

1. Stay True to Yourself: Your authenticity is your greatest asset as an influencer. Stay true to your values, passions, and voice, and let your unique personality shine through in everything you do. Embrace your quirks, flaws, and imperfections, and celebrate what makes you authentically you.

2. Embrace Growth and Learning: The journey of an influencer is a continuous process of growth, learning, and self-discovery. Be open to new experiences, perspectives, and opportunities for personal and professional development. Seek feedback, reflect on your experiences, and use every challenge as an opportunity to learn and grow.

3. Build Genuine Connections: Focus on building genuine connections with your audience, peers, and collaborators. Engage authentically, listen actively, and prioritize building meaningful relationships based on trust, respect, and mutual

support. Remember that behind every follower count is a real person with hopes, dreams, and struggles.

4. Stay Resilient and Persistent: Success as an influencer doesn't happen overnight. It requires resilience, persistence, and a willingness to persevere in the face of challenges and setbacks. Stay focused on your goals, stay resilient in the face of adversity, and keep pushing forward even when the journey feels challenging.

5. Celebrate Your Wins: Take time to celebrate your achievements, milestones, and successes along the way. Whether it's reaching a follower milestone, landing a coveted brand partnership, or receiving positive feedback from your audience, celebrate your wins and acknowledge the progress you've made on your journey.

6. Be Kind to Yourself: Remember to be kind to yourself and practice self-care as you navigate the ups and downs of your influencer journey. Take breaks when needed, prioritize your mental and emotional well-being, and surround yourself with a supportive network of friends, family, and fellow influencers who lift you up and encourage you to be your best self.

As you embark on your journey as an influencer, know that you are not alone. Countless others have walked this path before you, and many more will follow in your footsteps. Embrace the adventure, stay true to yourself, and trust in your ability to make a positive impact through your influence and authenticity.

Your journey as an influencer is uniquely yours, and I can't wait to see where it takes you. Remember to embrace every moment, cherish every experience, and never stop believing in the power of your voice and your story to inspire others.

With love and encouragement,

Vishal Raj Oberoi

www.ingramcontent.com/pod-product-compliance
Lightning Source LLC
LaVergne TN
LVHW051751050326
832903LV00029B/2849